Whistler Stories

Don C. Seitz

Contents

PREFACE 7
WHISTLER STORIES 8

WHISTLER STORIES

BY

Don C. Seitz

TO SHERIDAN FORD,

*DISCOVERER OF THE ART OF FOLLY
AND OF MANY FOLLIES OF ART*

PREFACE

Following the example set by Homer when he "smote his bloomin' lyre," as cited by Mr. Kipling, who went "an' took what he'd admire," I have gleaned the vast volume of Whistler literature and helped myself in making this compilation. Some few of the anecdotes are first-hand. Others were garnered by Mr. Ford in the original version of *The Gentle Art of Making Enemies*. The rest have been published many times, perhaps. But it seemed desirable to put the tales together without the distraction of other matter. So here they are.

D.C.S. Cos Cob, CONN.,
July, 1913.

WHISTLER STORIES

The studios of Chelsea are full of Whistler anecdotes. One tells of a female model to whom he owed some fifteen shillings for sittings. She was a Philistine of the Philistines who knew nothing of her patron's fame and was in no way impressed with his work. One day she told another artist that she had been sitting to a little Frenchman called Whistler, who jumped about his studio and was always complaining that people were swindling him, and that he was making very little money. The artist suggested that if she could get any piece of painting out of Whistler's studio he would give her ten pounds for it. Although skeptical, the model decided to tell her "little Frenchman" of this too generous offer, and selected one of the biggest and finest works in the studio. "What did he say?" asked the artist who had made the offer, when the model appeared in a state of great excitement and looking almost as if she had come second best out of a scrimmage. "He said, 'Ten pounds--Good heavens!--ten pounds!' and he got so mad--well, that's how I came in here like this."

* * * * *

Mr. W.P. Frith, R.A., following the custom of artists, talked to a model one day to keep her expression animated. He asked the girl to whom she had been sitting of late, and received the answer:
"Mr. Whistler."
"And did he talk to you?"
"Yes, sir."
"What did he say?"

"He asked me who I'd been sitting to, same as you do; and I told him I'd been sitting to Mr. Cope, sir."

"Well, what else?"

"He asked me who I'd been sitting to before that, and I said Mr. Horsley."

"And what next?"

"He asked me who I'd been sitting to before that, and I said I'd been sitting to you, sir."

"What did he say then?"

"He said, 'What a d----d crew!'"

* * * * *

Whistler once came very near painting a portrait of Disraeli. He had the commission; he even went down to the country where Disraeli was; but the great man did not manage to get into the mood. Whistler departed disappointed, and shortly afterward took place a meeting in Whitehall which was the occasion of a well-known story: Disraeli put his arm in Whistler's for a little way on the street, bringing from the artist the exclamation, "If only my creditors could see!"

* * * * *

Whistler's ideas, the reverse of commercial, not infrequently placed him in want. He pawned his portrait of his mother, by many considered the best of his productions.

Miss Marion Peck, a niece of Ferdinand Peck, United States Commissioner to the Paris Exposition, wanted her portrait done by Whistler. She sat for him nineteen times. Further, she requested, as the picture was nearing completion, that extra pains be taken with its finishing. Also, she inquired if it could, without danger of injury, be shipped.

"Why?" asked Whistler.

"Because I wish to send it to my home in Chicago," explained Miss Peck.

Whistler threw down his brush, overturned the easel, and ran around the studio like a madman. "What!" he shrieked. "Send a Whistler to Chicago! Allow one of my paintings to enter Hog Town! Never!"

Miss Peck didn't get the painting.

* * * * *

Once he met what seemed to be a crushing retort. He had scornfully called Balaam's ass the first great critic, and the inference was plain until a writer in *Vanity Fair* called his attention to the fact that the ass was right.

Whistler acknowledged the point. But the acknowledgment terminates in a way that is delicious. "I fancy you will admit that this is the only ass on record who ever did 'see the Angel of the Lord,' and that we are past the age of miracles."

Even in defeat he was triumphant.

* * * * *

Whistler found that Mortimer Menpes, once his very dear friend, sketched in Chelsea. "How dare you sketch in my Chelsea?" he indignantly demanded.

A vigorous attack on Mr. Menpes then followed in the press. One of the first articles began in this style, Menpes, of course, being an Australian: "I can only liken him to his native kangaroo--a robber by birth--born with a pocket!" "He is the claimant of lemon yellow"--a color to which Mr. Whistler deemed he had the sole right; and when he thought he had pulverized him in the press (it was soon after the Parnell Commission, when Pigott, the informer, had committed suicide in Spain), Whistler one evening thrust this pleasant note into Mr. Menpes's letter-box, scrawled on a half-sheet of paper, with the well-known butterfly cipher attached:

"You will blow your brains out, of course. Pigott has shown you what to do under the circumstances, and you know the way to Spain. Good-by!"

Speaking at a meeting held to complete the details of a movement for the erection of a memorial to Whistler, Lord Redesdale gave a remarkable account of the artist's methods of work. "One day when he was to begin a portrait of a lady," said Lord Redesdale, "the painter took up his position at one end of the room, with his sitter and canvas at the other. For a long time he stood looking at her, holding in his hand a huge brush as a man would use to whitewash a house. Suddenly he ran forward and smashed the brush full of color upon the canvas. Then he ran back, and forty or fifty times he repeated this. At the end of that time there stood out on the canvas a space which exactly indicated the figure and the expression of his sitter."

This portrait was to have belonged to Lord Redesdale, but through circumstances nothing less than tragic it never came into his possession. There were bailiffs in the house when it was finished. This was no novelty to Whistler. He only laughed, and, laughing, made a circuit of his studio with a palette-knife, deliberately destroying all the pictures exposed there. The portrait of the lady was among them.

* * * * *

Moncure D. Conway in his autobiography relates this:
"At a dinner given to W.J. Stillman, at which Whistler (a Confederate) related with satisfaction his fisticuffs with a Yankee on shipboard, William Rossetti remarked: 'I must say, Whistler, that your conduct was scandalous.' Stillman and myself were silent. Dante Gabriel Rossetti promptly wrote:

"'There is a young artist called Whistler,
  Who in every respect is a bristler;
    A tube of white lead
    Or a punch on the head
  Come equally handy to Whistler.'"

On one occasion a woman said to Whistler:
"I just came up from the country this morning along the Thames, and there was an exquisite haze in the atmosphere which reminded me so much of some of your little things. It was really a perfect series of Whistlers."

"Yes, madam," responded Whistler, gravely. "Nature is creeping up."

* * * * *

Richard A. Canfield, who sat for the portrait now called "His Reverence," though Canfield was something quite unclerical, recites:

"After I had my first sitting on New Year's Day, 1903, I saw Whistler every day until the day I sailed for New York, which was on May 16th. He was not able to work, however, on all those days. In fact, there were days at a time when he could do nothing but lie on a couch and talk, as only Whistler could talk, about those things which interested him. It was mostly of art and artists that he conversed, but now and again he would revert to his younger days at home, to the greatness to which the republic had attained, and to his years at West Point.

"In spite of all that has been said of him, I know that James McNeill Whistler was one of the intensest Americans who ever lived. He was not what you call an enthusiastic man, but when he reverted to the old days at the Military Academy his enthusiasm was infectious. I think he was really prouder of the years he spent there--three, I think they were--than any other years of his life. He never tired of telling of the splendid men and soldiers his classmates turned out to be, and he has often said to me that the American army officer trained at West Point was the finest specimen of manhood and of honor in the world.

"It was in this way that I spent every afternoon with Whistler from New Year's until May 15th, the day before I sailed. When he was able to work I would sit as I was told, and then he would paint, sometimes an hour, sometimes three. At other times he would lie on the couch and ask me to sit by and talk to him. On the morning of the day of the last sitting he sent me a note asking me to take luncheon with him, and Adding that he felt quite himself and up to plenty of work.

"So I went around to his studio, and he painted until well into the late afternoon. When he was done he said that with a touch or two here and there the picture might be considered finished. Then he added:

"'You are going home to-morrow, to my home as well as yours, and you won't be coming back till the autumn. I've just been thinking that maybe you had better take the picture along with you. His Reverence will do very well as he is, and maybe there won't be any work in me when you come back. I believe I would rather like to think of you having this clerical gentleman in your collection, for I have a notion that it's the best work I have done.'

"Whistler had never talked that way before, and I have since thought that he was thinking that the end was not far away. I told him, more to get the notion, if he had it, out of his mind than anything else, that I would not think of taking the picture, and that if he didn't put on one of those finishing touches until I got back, so much the better, for then I could see him work. That seemed to bring him back to himself, and he said:

"'So be it, your Reverence. Now we'll say *au revoir* in a couple of mint-juleps.' He sent for the materials, made the cups, and, just as the sun was setting, we drank to each other and the homeland, and I was off to catch a train for Liverpool and the steamer. So it was that Whistler and his last subject parted."

*　*　*　*　*

A group of American and English artists were discussing the manifold perfections of the late Lord Leighton, president of the Royal Academy.

"Exquisite musician--played the violin like a professional," said one.

"One of the best-dressed men in London," said another.

"Danced divinely," remarked the third.

"Ever read his essays?" asked a fourth. "In my opinion they're the best of the kind ever written."

Whistler, who had remained silent, tapped the last speaker on the shoulder.

"Painted, too, didn't he?" he said.

*　*　*　*　*

A patron of art asked Whistler to tell him where a friend lived on a certain street in London, to which the artist replied:

"I can't tell you, but I know how you can find it. Just you ring up houses until you come across a caretaker who talks in B flat, and there you are."

* * * * *

A friend of Whistler's saw him on the street in London a few years ago talking to a very ragged little newsboy. As he approached to speak to the artist he noticed that the boy was as dirty a specimen of the London "newsy" as he had ever encountered--he seemed smeared all over--literally covered with dirt.

Whistler had just asked him a question, and the boy answered:

"Yes, sir; I've been selling papers three years."

"How old are you?" inquired Whistler.

"Seven, sir."

"Oh, you must be more than that."

"No, sir, I ain't."

Then, turning to his friend, who had overheard the conversation, Whistler said: "I don't think he could get that dirty in seven years; do you?"

* * * * *

Benrimo, the dramatist, who wrote "The Yellow Jacket," relates that when he was a young writer, fresh from the breezy atmosphere of San Francisco, he visited London. Coming out of the Burlington Gallery one day, he saw a little man mincing toward him, carrying a cane held before him as he walked, whom he recognized as Whistler. With Western audacity he stopped the pedestrian, introduced himself, and broke into an elaborate outburst of acclamation for the works of the master, who "ate it up," as the saying goes.

Waving his wand gently toward the famous gallery, Whistler queried:

"Been in there?"

"Oh, yes."

"See anything worth while?"

"Some splendid things, magnificent examples--"

"I'm sorry you ever approved of me," observed the master, majestically, and on he went, leaving Benrimo withered under his disdain.

* * * * *

Whistler had a French poodle of which he was extravagantly fond. This poodle was seized with an affection of the throat, and Whistler had the audacity to send for the great throat specialist, Mackenzie. Sir Morell, when he saw that he had been called to treat a dog, didn't like it much, it was plain. But he said nothing. He prescribed, pocketed a big fee, and drove away. The next day he sent posthaste for Whistler. And Whistler, thinking he was summoned on some matter connected with his beloved dog, dropped his work and rushed like the wind to Mackenzie's. On his arrival Sir Morell said, gravely: "How do you do, Mr. Whistler? I wanted to see you about having my front door painted."

* * * * *

Whistler used to tell this story about Dante Gabriel Rossetti in his later years. The great Pre-Raphaelite had invited the painter of nocturnes and harmonies to dine with him at his house in Chelsea, and when Whistler arrived he was shown into a reception-room. Seating himself, he was soon disturbed by a noise which appeared to be made by a rat or a mouse in the wainscoting of the room. This surmise was wrong, as he found the noise was in the center of the apartment. Stooping, to his amazement he saw Rossetti lying at full length under the table.

"Why, what on earth are you doing there, Rossetti?" exclaimed Whistler.

"Don't speak to me! Don't speak to me!" cried Rossetti. "That fool Morris"-- meaning the famous William--"has sent to say he can't dine here to-night, and I'm so mad I'm gnawing the leg of the table."

* * * * *

One of the affectations of Whistler was his apparent failure to recognize persons with whom he had been on the most friendly terms. An American artist once met the impressionist in Venice, where they spent several months together painting, and he was invited to call on Whistler if he should go to Paris. The painter remembered the invitation. The door of the Paris studio was opened by Whistler himself. A cold stare was the only reply to the visitor's effusive greeting.

"Why, Mr. Whistler," cried the painter, "you surely haven't forgotten those days in Venice when you borrowed my colors and we painted together!"

"I never saw you before in all my life," replied Whistler, and slammed the door.

This habit of forgetting persons, or pretending to do so, for nobody ever knew when the lapses of recognition were due to intention or absent-mindedness, often tempted other artists to play pranks upon him. He was a man who resented a joke at his own expense, except on a few occasions, and this trait was often turned to good account.

He was at Naples soon after the incident just related had gained wide circulation. A conspiracy was entered into whereby the Whistler worshipers there were to be unaware of his presence. He tried to play billiards with a company of young artists. They met his advance with a stony glare.

"Oh, I say," persisted he, "I think I know something of that game. I'd like to play."

A consultation was held, and the artists shook their heads, inquiring of one another, "Who is he?" Whistler retired crestfallen, and a roar of laughter which rang through the room added to his discomfiture.

"Oh, well," he said, pulling nervously at his mustache, and his tone was petulant, "I don't care."

* * * * *

Whistler had a great penchant for white hats, kept all those he had ever worn, and had a large collection. The flat-brimmed tall hat was a whim of his late years, imported from France, ***via*** the head of William M. Chase.

* * * * *

Mr. Chase has contributed largely to the budget of Whistler anecdotes. One day when the two men were painting together in Whistler's studio in London, a wealthy woman visited them with the demand, which she had made many times before, that Whistler return to her a picture by himself which he had borrowed several years before to place on exhibition. The suave voice of Whistler was heard in argument, and he finally induced his patron to depart without the work of art.

When she had gone he returned to his work, muttering something about the absurdity of some persons who believed that because they had paid two hundred pounds for a picture they thought they thereby owned it.

"Besides," he said, "there is absolutely nothing else in her house to compare with it, and it would be out of place."

* * * * *

"Chase," said Whistler one day, "how-is it now in America? Do you find there, as you do in London, that in houses filled with beautiful pictures and superb statuary, and other objects of artistic merit, there is invariably some damned little thing on the mantel that gives the whole thing away?" Mr. Chase replied, sadly: "It is even so, but you must remember, Whistler, that there are such things as birthdays. People are not always responsible."

* * * * *

Mr. Chase came up for discussion once at a little party, and Whistler's sister observed, "Mr. Chase amuses James, doesn't he, James?" James, tapping his fingertips together lightly: "Not often, not often."

* * * * *

"I'm going over to London," said he once to Chase, "and there I shall have a hansom made. It shall have a white body, yellow wheels, and I'll have it lined with canary-colored satin. I'll petition the city to let me carry one lamp on it, and on the lamp there will be a white plume. I shall then be the only one."

He gave Mr. Chase some pretty hard digs. He said to him one time in the heat of a discussion on some technical point: "Chase, I am not arguing with you. I am telling you."

* * * * *

Reproved by Mr. Chase for antagonizing his friends, Whistler retorted:

"It is commonplace, not to say vulgar, to quarrel with your enemies. Quarrel with your friends! That's the thing to do. Now be good!"

* * * * *

"The good Lord made one serious mistake," he rasped to Chase, in Holland. "What?"

"When he made Dutchmen."

* * * * *

When he had finished his portrait of Mr. Chase he stood off and admired the work. "Beautiful! Beautiful!" was his comment. Chase, who had irked under the queer companionship, retorted, "At least there's nothing mean or modest about you!"

"Nothing mean and modest," he corrected. "I like that better! Nothing mean ***and*** modest! What a splendid epitaph that would make for me! Stop a moment! I must put that down!"

* * * * *

During the Chase sittings, the creditors were always calling. Whistler divined their several missions with much nicety by the tone of the raps on the door.

A loud, business-like bang brought, out this comment:

"Psst! That's one and ten."

Later came another, not quite so vehement.

"Two and six," said Whistler. "Psst!"

"What on earth do you mean?" asked Chase.

"One pound ten shillings; two pounds six shillings! Vulgar tradesmen with their bills, Colonel. They want payment. Oh, well!"

A gentle knock soon followed.

"Dear me," said Whistler, "that must be all of twenty! Poor fellow! I really must do something for him. So sorry I'm not in."

* * * * *

Riding one day in a hansom with Mr. Chase, Whistler's eye caught the fruit and vegetable display in a greengrocer's shop. Making the cabby maneuver the vehicle to various viewpoints, he finally observed: "Isn't it beautiful? I believe I'll have that crate of oranges moved over there--against that background of green. Yes, that's better!" And he settled back contentedly!

A kindly friend told him of a pleasant spot near London for an artistic sojourn. "I'm sure you'll like it," he added, enthusiastically.

"My dear fellow," replied Whistler, "the very fact that you like it is proof that it's nothing for me."

He went, however, and liked the place, but on the way some of his canvases went astray. He made such a fuss that the station-master asked Mr. Chase who was his companion: "Who is that quarrelsome little man? He's really most disagreeable."

"Whistler, the celebrated artist," Mr. Chase replied.

At that the man approached Whistler and respectfully remarked:

"I'm very sorry about your canvases. Are they valuable?"

"Not yet!" screeched Whistler. "Not yet!"

"I only know of two painters in the world," said a newly introduced feminine enthusiast to Whistler, "yourself and Velasquez."

"Why," answered Whistler, in dulcet tones, "why drag in Velasquez?"

Mr. Chase once asked him if he really said this seriously.

"No, of course not," he replied. "You don't suppose I couple myself with Velasquez, do you? I simply wanted to take her down."

* * * * *

Sir John E. Millais, walking through the Grosvenor Gallery with Archibald Stuart Wortley, stopped longer than usual before the shadowy, graceful portrait of a lady, "an arrangement in gray, rose, and silver," and then broke out: "It's damned clever! It's a damned sight too clever!"

This was his verdict on Whistler's portrait of Lady Meux. Millais contended that Whistler "never learned the grammar of his art," that "his drawing is as faulty as it can be," and that "he thought nothing" of depicting "a woman all out of proportion, with impossible legs and arms!"

* * * * *

In 1874 there was a suggestion that Whistler's portrait of Carlyle should be bought for the National Gallery. Sir George Scharf, then curator of that institution, came to Mr. Graves's show-rooms in Pall Mall to take a look at it.

When Mr. Graves produced the painting he observed, icily:

"Well, and has painting come to this?"

"I told Mr. Graves," said Whistler, "that he should have said,' No, it hasn't.'"

It was nearly twenty years after when Glasgow finally bought the masterpiece. Indeed, Whistler had little market for his works until 1892.

He often found, as he said, "a long face and a short account at the bank." Complaining to Sidney Starr one day of the sums earned by a certain eminent "R.A.," while he received little or nothing, Starr reminded him that R.A.'s painted to please the public and so reaped their reward.

"I don't think they do," demurred Whistler; "I think they paint as well as they can."

Of Alma-Tadema's work he observed, "My only objection to Tadema's pictures is that they are unfinished."

Starr spoke approvingly of the promising work of some of the younger artists. "They are all tarred with the same brush," said Whistler. "They are of the schools!" Of one particular rising star Whistler remarked: "He's clever, but there's something common in everything he does. So what's the use of it?"

Starr indicated a distinguishing difference between the work of a certain R.A. and another. "Well," he replied, "it's a nasty difference."

* * * * *

M.H. Spielmann, the art-critic, spoke of "Ten o'Clock " as "smart but misleading." Whistler retorted, "If the lecture had not seemed misleading to him, it surely would not have been worth uttering at all!"

* * * * *

Walter Sickert, then a pupil of Whistler's, praised Lord Leighton's "Harvest Moon" in an article on the Manchester Art Treasure Exhibition. Whistler telegraphed him at Hampstead:

"The Harvest Moon rises at Hampstead and the cocks of Chelsea crow!"

* * * * *

Apropos of his spats with Sickert he remarked, "Yes, we are always forgiving Walter."

Another pupil, foreseeing the end of Whistler as president of the Royal Society of British Artists, resigned some months before the time. "The early rat," said Whistler, grimly, "the first to leave the sinking ship."

* * * * *

In the Fine Art Society's gallery one day he spoke to a knighted R.A. "Who was that?" Starr asked.

"Really, now, I forget," was the reply. "But whoever it was it's some one of no importance, you know, no importance whatever."

* * * * *

At an exhibition of Doré's pictures Whistler asked an attendant if a certain academician's large religious picture was not on view.

"No," said the man; "it's much lower down!"

"Impossible!" replied Whistler, gleefully.

Sidney Starr relates that Whistler was asked one year to "hang" the exhibits in the Walker Art Gallery at Liverpool. In the center of one wall he placed Luke Fildes's "Doctor," and surrounded it with all the pictures he could find of dying people, convalescents, still-life medicine bottles, and the like. This caused comment. "But," said Whistler, "I told them I wished to emphasize that particular school."

"And what did you put on the opposite wall?" Starr asked.

"Oh, Leighton's--I really forget what it was."

"But that is different, you know," said Starr.

"No," rejoined Whistler; "it's really the same thing!"

* * * * *

Having seen a picture of Starr's in Liverpool, which he amiably, termed "a picture among paint," he observed to him on the occasion of their first meeting: "Paint things exactly as they are. I always do. Young men think they should paint like this or that painter. Be quite simple; no fussy foolishness, you know; and don't try to be what they call 'strong.' When a picture 'smells of paint,'" he said slowly, "it's what they call 'strong.'"

* * * * *

Riding once with Starr to dine at the Café Royal, Whistler leaned forward in the hansom and looked at the green park in the dusk, fresh and sweet after the rain; at the long line of light reflected, shimmering, in the wet Piccadilly pavement, and said:

"Starr, I have not dined, as you know, so you need not think I say this in anything but a cold and careful spirit: it is better to live on bread and cheese and paint beautiful things than to live like Dives and paint pot-boilers. But a painter really should not have to worry about--'various,' you know. Poverty may induce industry, but it does not produce the fine flower of painting. The test is not poverty; it's money. Give a painter money and see what he'll do. If he does not paint, his work is well lost to the world. If I had had, say, three thousand pounds a year, what beautiful things I could have done!"

* * * * *

Before the portrait of little Miss Alexander went to the Grosvenor Gallery, Tom Taylor, the art-critic of the *Times*, called at the studio to see it. "Ah, yes--'um," he remarked, and added that an upright line in the paneling of the wall was wrong and that the picture would be better without it, adding, "Of course, it's a matter of taste."

To which Whistler rejoined: "I thought that perhaps for once you were going to get away without having said anything foolish; but remember, so you may not make the mistake again, it's not a matter of taste at all; it is a matter of knowledge. Good-by!"

* * * * *

To a critic who remarked, "Your picture is not up to your mark; it is not good this time," Whistler replied: "You shouldn't say it is not good. You should say you do not like it, and then, you know, you're perfectly safe. Now come and have something you do like--have some whiskey."

* * * * *

Stopped at an exhibition by an attendant who wished to check his cane, Whistler laughed: "Oh, no, my little man; I keep this for the critics."

His troubles with the Royal Society of British Artists bred a round of biting remarks. When he and his following went out he said, consolingly: "Pish! It is very simple. The artists retired. The British remained!"

Another shot at the same subject:

"No longer can it be said that the right man is in the wrong place!"

* * * * *

When an adverse vote ended his leadership of the Royal Society, Whistler said, philosophically, "Now I understand the feelings of all those who, since the world began, have tried to save their fellow-men."

* * * * *

Commenting on B.R. Haydon's autobiography, Whistler said: "Yes; Haydon, it seems, went into his studio, locked the door, and before beginning to work prayed God to enable him to paint for the glory of England. Then, seizing a large brush full of bitumen, he attacked his huge canvas, and, of course--God fled."

* * * * *

Starr once asked Whistler if the southern exposure of the room in which he was working troubled him.

"Yes, it does," he answered. "But Ruskin lives in the North, you know, and a southern exposure troubled him, rather, eh?"

* * * * *

Much that was characteristic of the artist's wit and temper came out during the famous libel suit he brought against Ruskin. The most amusing feature of it was the exhibition in court of some of the "nocturnes" and "arrangements" which were the subject of the suit. The jury of respectable citizens, whose knowledge of art was probably limited, was expected to pass judgment on these paintings. Whistler's counsel held up one of the pictures.

"Here, gentlemen," he said, "is one of the works which have been maligned."

"Pardon me," interposed Mr. Ruskin's lawyer; "you have that picture upside down."

"No such thing!"

"Oh, but it is so!" continued Ruskin's counsel. "I remember it in the Grosvenor Gallery, where it was hung the other way about."

The altercation ended in the correctness of view of Ruskin's lawyer being sustained. This error of counsel helped to produce the celebrated farthing verdict. Ever after Whistler wore the farthing on his watch-chain.

* * * * *

The suit had its origin in Ruskin's comment upon the "Nocturne in Black and Gold," described as "a distant view of Cremorne Garden, with a falling rocket and other fireworks." The picture is now the property of Mrs. Samuel Untermyer, of New York. On the opening of the Grosvenor Gallery, in 1877, Ruskin wrote in **Fors Clavigera**: "The ill-educated conceit of the artist nearly approached the aspect of wilful imposture. I have seen and heard much of cockney impudence before now, but never expected to have a coxcomb ask two hundred guineas for flinging a pot of paint in the public's face."

When Whistler was being examined during the trial, Sir John Holker, the Attorney-General, asked, "How long did it take you to knock off that 'Nocturne'?"

"I beg your pardon?" said the witness.

Sir John apologized for his flippancy, and Whistler replied: "About a day. I may have put a few touches to it the next day."

"For two days' labor you ask two hundred guineas?"

"No, I ask it for the knowledge of a lifetime!"

Then the "Nocturne in Blue and Silver," a moonlight view of Battersea Bridge, was submitted to the jury. Baron Huddleston, the presiding justice, asked Mr. Whistler to explain it.

"Which part of the picture is the bridge?" he queried. "Do you say this is a correct representation?"

"I did not intend it to be a correct portrait of the bridge."

"Are the figures on the top intended for people?"

"They are just what you like."

"Is that a barge beneath?"

"Yes," replied the witness, sarcastically. "I am much encouraged at your perceiving that! My whole scheme was only to bring out a certain harmony of color."

"What is that gold-colored mark on the side, like a cascade?"

"That is a firework."

"Do you think now," said the Attorney-General, insinuatingly, "you could make me see the beauty of that picture?"

"No," said Whistler, after closely scrutinizing his questioner's face. "Do you know, I fear it would be as hopeless as for the musician to pour his notes into a deaf man's ear."

"What is that structure in the middle?" asked the irritated attorney. "Is it a telescope or a fire-escape? Is it like Battersea Bridge? What are the figures at the top? If they are horses and carts, how in the name of fortune are they to get off?"

*   *   *   *   *

A friend who was in court when the farthing damages verdict was brought in relates that Whistler looked puzzled for a moment; then his face cleared. "That's a verdict for me, is it not?" he asked; and when his counsel said, "Yes, nominally," Whistler replied, "Well, I suppose a verdict is a verdict." Then he said, "It's a great triumph; tell everybody it's a great triumph." When the listener dissented, he condensed all his concentrated scorn of Philistine view into a sentence: "My dear S., you are just fit to serve on a British jury."

* * * * *

"Whistler *vs.* Ruskin" cost the latter so much more than the farthing verdict that his friends sent out a circular soliciting funds in these terms:

"Whistler *vs.* Ruskin. Mr. Ruskin's costs.

"A considerable opinion prevailing that a lifelong, honest endeavor on the part of Mr. Ruskin to further the cause of Art should not be crowned by his being cast in costs to the amount of several hundreds of pounds, the Fine Art Society has agreed to set on foot a subscription to defray his expenses arising out of the late action of Whistler *vs.* Ruskin.

"Persons willing to co-operate will oblige by communicating with the Society, 148, New Bond Street, London."

Mr. Whistler received scant sympathy, the tone of the comment being well noted by this excerpt from the London **Standard** of November 30th, 1878:

"Of course, Mr. Whistler has costs to pay too, and the amount he is to receive from Mr. Ruskin (one farthing), even if economically expended, will hardly go far to satisfy the claims of his legal advisers. But he has only to paint, or, as we believe he expresses it, 'knock off,' three or four 'symphonies' or 'harmonies'--or perhaps he might try his hand at a Set of Quadrilles in Peacock Blue?--and a week's labor will set all square."

Arthur Lumley, a New York illustrator, met Whistler once at a costume ball at George H. Boughton's house in London. The artist appeared as Hamlet, but in anything but a melancholy mood. Next morning's papers related that the sheriff had sold the effects in the White House the day of the ball to satisfy the claims of his creditors!

* * * * *

Isaac N. Ford, when correspondent of the New York **Tribune** in London, went with Frederick MacMonnies, the sculptor, to visit Whistler, who brought out a number of portraits for show. One was that of a woman, full figure.

"What do you think of her?" he asked.

The sculptor gave "a side glance and looked down."

"Since you force me to speak,", he finally blurted out, "I must tell you that one leg is longer than the other."

Instead of the expected outburst, Whistler scrutinized the portrait from several points, and then observed quietly:

"You are quite right. I had not observed the fault, and I shall correct it in the morning."

"What an eye for a line a sculptor has!" he said to Ford later.

* * * * *

He quarreled regularly with his brother-in-law, Sir F. Seymour Haden, the famous etcher.

"A brother-in-law is not a connection calling for sentiment," he once remarked.

Haden came into a gallery on one occasion and, seeing Whistler, who was there in company with Justice Day, left abruptly.

"I see! Dropped in for his morning bitters," observed Whistler, cheerfully.

* * * * *

Once in conversation Whistler said: "Yes, I have many friends, and am grateful to them; but those whom I most love are my enemies--not in a Biblical sense, oh, no, but because they keep one always busy, always up to the mark, either fighting them or proving them idiots."

* * * * *

Whistler was very particular about the spelling of his rather long and complicated group of names. Careless people made the "Mc" "Mac," and others left the extra "l" off "McNeill." To one of the latter offenders he wrote:

"McNeill, by the way, should have two l's.' I use them both, and in the midst of things cannot well do without them!"

* * * * *

When Tom Taylor, the critic, died, a friend asked Whistler why he looked so glum.

"Me?" said Whistler. "Who else has such cause to mourn? Tommy's dead. I'm lonesome. They are all dying. I have hardly a warm personal enemy left!"

* * * * *

While a draughtsman in the Coast Survey from November, 1854, to February, 1855, he boarded at the northeast corner of E and 12th Streets, Washington. He is remembered as being usually late for breakfast and always making sketches on the walls. To the remonstrating landlord he replied:

"Now, now, never mind! I'll not charge you anything for the decorations."

* * * * *

Among those with whom Whistler quarreled most joyously were the two Moores, the illustrious George and his less famous brother, Augustus. Both took Sir William Eden's side in the celebrated "Baronet *vs*. Butterfly" case, where Whistler was nonsuited in a French court of law. Augustus edited a sprightly but none too reputable weekly in London, called the ***Hawk***, a series of unpalatable references in which so aroused Whistler that, meeting Moore in the Drury Lane Theater on the first night of "A Million of Money," he struck the editor across the face with his cane. A scrimmage followed, which contemporary history closed with the artist on the floor. Whistler's own account of the unseemly fracas was thuswise:

"I started out to cane the fellow with as little emotion as I would prepare to kill a rat. I did cane him to the satisfaction of my many friends and his many enemies, and that was the end of it."

Moore wrote: "I am sorry, but I have had to slap Mr. Whistler. My Irish blood got the better of me, and before I knew it the shriveled-up little monkey was knocked over and kicking about the floor."

Whistler vigorously controverted this version as a "barefaced falsehood." He added: "I am sure he never touched me. I don't know why, for he is a much bigger man than I. My idea is that he was thoroughly cowed by the moral force of my attack. I had to turn him round in order to get at him. Then I cut him again and again as hard as I could, hissing out 'Hawk!' with each stroke. Oh, you can take my word for it, everything was done in the cleanest and most correct fashion possible. I always like to do things cleanly."

* * * * *

The clash with George Moore came to a head with the challenge to fight a duel. In his own version of the event given in the London ***Chronicle*** of March 29th, 1895, Mr. Moore laid his troubles to his efforts to aid the artist. Learning that Sir William Eden wished his wife's portrait painted, he "undertook a journey to Paris in the depth of winter, had two shocking passages across the Channel, and spent twenty-five pounds on Mr. Whistler's business." It was arranged, he thought, that Whistler was to receive one hundred pounds for a "small sketch." When the "sketch" materialized it was "small" indeed. The Baronet and Mr. Moore expected a little more area of canvas. "The picture in question," remarked Mr. Moore, "is only twelve inches long by six high. The figure of Lady Eden is represented sitting on a sofa; the face is about half an inch in length, about the size of a sixpence, and the features are barely indicated."

But to the duel: In Paris, after the controversy arose, Mr. Moore told an interviewer he did not think the sketch was worth more than one hundred pounds. To this Whistler made a furious reply in the ***Pall Mall Gazette***, alleging that Moore had "acquired a spurious reputation as an art-critic" by praising his pictures. Moore's reply in the journal produced this response, sent from the Hotel Chatham under date of March 12th, 1895:

"Mr. Whistler begs to acknowledge Mr. Moore's letter of March 11.

"If, in it, the literary incarnation of the 'eccentric' person, on the curbstone, is supposed to represent Mr. Moore at the present moment, Mr. Whistler thinks the likeness exaggerated--as it is absurd to suppose that Mr. Moore can really imagine that any one admires him in his late role before Interviewer, or in that of the Expert in the Council Chamber.

"If, however, Mr. Moore means in his parable to indicate Mr. Whistler, the latter is willing to accept Mr. Moore's circuitous and coarse attempt to convey a gross insult--and, upon the whole, will perhaps think the better of him for an intention to make himself at last responsible.

"In such case Mr. Whistler will ask a friend to meet any gentleman Mr. Moore may appoint to represent him; and, awaiting a reply, has the honor to remain Mr. Moore's," etc.

To which Mr. Moore replied:

"Mr. Moore begs to acknowledge the receipt of Mr. Whistler's letter of the 12th inst. In Mr. Moore's opinion Mr. Whistler's conduct grows daily more absurd."

"I hoped," explained Mr. Moore, "that Mr. Whistler's friends would intervene and persuade him of the strangeness of his action and the interpretation it would receive in England. But four days later I was flattered by the following communication:

"PARIS, ***le 15 Mars, 1895.***
"MONSIEUR:
"A la réception de votre lettre (lettre d'ailleurs rendue publique dans la ***Pall Mall Gazette***), M. Whistler nous a prié de vous demander soit une rétractation, soit

une réparation par les armes.

"Nous vous prions donc de vouloir bien nous mettre en rapport avec deux de vos amis.

FRANCIS VIELÉ-GRIFFIN,

122 Rue de la Pompe. OCTAVE MIRBEAU, Carrière-sous-Passy, Seine-et-Oise."

Mr. Moore's interlocutor asked him if there was any fear of losing his interesting personality on account of Mr. Whistler's challenge.

To this Mr. Moore said:

"There are three most excellent reasons why I should not fight a duel with Mr. Whistler, as Mr. Whistler well knows. First, only under the very gravest circumstances, if under any at all, would an Englishman accept a challenge to a duel. The duel has been relegated to the realms of comic opera. As for inviting me to proceed to Belgium for the purpose of fighting him, he might as well ask me to strip myself naked and paint my face and stick feathers in my hair--dress myself as a Redskin, in fact, and walk down St. James's Street flourishing a tomahawk. Second, supposing I were a Frenchman, Mr. Whistler is sixty-five years of age, and it is against the custom of dueling for any one to accept a challenge from so old a gentleman. Moreover, Mr. Whistler is, unhappily, very short-sighted, and would be unable to see me at twenty paces. Third, the grounds of the quarrel are so infinitely trivial that, were we both Frenchmen, it is doubtful if any seconds would take upon themselves the responsibility of an armed encounter.

"I have praised Mr. Whistler's pictures that he painted five-and-twenty years ago as much as it is possible to praise works of art. I hold the same opinions about them still. I only wish Mr. Whistler would apply himself to his art instead of wasting his time in quarreling with his friends."

The outcome of the Eden suit kept Whistler in ill-humor for a long time, while Moore continued to be a special object of aversion. The two avoided each other. But, as some philosopher has said, if you remain long in Paris you will meet all your friends and all your enemies. So it fell out that the two foregathered at the same atelier one Sunday afternoon. They nearly collided in entering, but Moore was the first inside. The hostess heard sounds from the hall something between china-breaking and the stamping of hoofs. She went out, to find James in a mighty rage.

"Dear me!" said the lady, "what is the matter, dear master?"

"Whistler won't come in! Whistler won't stay under the same roof with that wild Irishman!"

Moore, in the inside, remarked in his sweetly modulated voice:

"Why drag in Whistler?"

This play on his best *mot*, "Why drag in Velasquez?" was too much, and in screaming wrath the painter fled, leaving Moore in full possession.

* * * * *

An American millionaire, to whom wealth had come rather quickly from Western mines, called at the Paris studio with the idea of capturing something for his gallery. He glanced casually at the paintings on the walls, and then queried:

"How much for the lot?"

"Four millions," said Whistler.

"What?"

"My posthumous prices! Good morning!"

* * * * *

Dante Gabriel Rossetti once showed Whistler a sketch and asked his opinion of its merits.

"It has good points, Rossetti," said Whistler. "Go ahead with it by all means."

Later he inquired how it was getting along. "All right," answered Rossetti, cheerfully. "I've ordered a stunning frame for it."

In due time the canvas appeared at Rossetti's house in Cheyne Walk, beautifully framed.

"You've done nothing to it since I saw it, have you?" said Whistler.

"No-o," replied Rossetti, "but I've written a sonnet on the subject, if you'd like to hear it."

He recited some lines of peculiar tenderness.

"Rossetti," said Whistler, as the recitation ended, "take out the picture and frame the sonnet."

* * * * *

The Scotch once raised a fund by subscription to buy the portrait of Carlyle, at a price of five hundred guineas, fixed by the painter. When the sum was nearly complete, he learned that the subscription paper contained a clause disclaiming any indorsement of his theory of art. He telegraphed to the committee:

"The price of 'Carlyle' has advanced to one thousand guineas. Dinna ye hear the bagpipes?"

* * * * *

A dilettante collector in London, after much angling, induced Whistler to view his variegated collection. As the several objects passed in review they provoked only a sober "H'm, h'm," that might have meant anything or nothing. When there was no more to see, the host paused for an aggregate opinion and got this:

"My dear sir, there's really no excuse for it, no excuse for it at all!"

To a lady who complained that the frequent sittings commanded for painting her portrait compelled her to sacrifice much personal convenience, Whistler replied: "But, my dear lady, that is nothing in comparison with the sacrifice I have to make on your account. Just look: since I have been painting your portrait I have not had time to attend to my correspondence."

There was a mountain of unopened letters on his desk.

* * * * *

Frederick Wedmore, the patient cataloguer of Whistler's etchings, once appeared in print as saying that he had "no wish to understand Whistler's works." He wrote "understate," but the wretched compositor undid him. Whistler's response to the explanation was: "Yes, the mistake is indeed inexcusable, since not only I, but even the compositor, might have known that with Mr. Wedmore and his like it is always a question of understating and never of understanding anything."

In his *Memories and Impressions* Ford Madox Hueffer relates that Madox Brown, going to a tea-party at the White House at Chelsea, was met in the hall by Mrs. Whistler, who begged him to go to the poulterer's and purchase a pound of butter. The bread was cut, but there was nothing in the house to put upon it. There was no money in the house, the poulterer had cut off his credit, and Mrs. Whistler said she dared not send her husband, for he would certainly punch the tradesman's head!

"To think of 'Arry [meaning Harry Quilter, the critic, with whom he fiercely quarreled] living in the temple I erected!" he said. "He has no use for it--doesn't know what to do with it. If he had any feeling for the sympathy of things he would come to me and say: 'Here's your house, Whistler; take it; you know its meaning, I don't. Take it and live in it.' But no, he hasn't sense enough to see that. He obstinately stays there in the way, while I am living in this absurd fashion, next door to myself."

* * * * *

After the "secession" from the Royal Society, Whistler strolled into the gallery one evening with some friends. A group of admirers were gushing before a Leighton canvas.

"Quite exquisite!"

"A gem--really a gem!"

"Yes," said Whistler. "Like a diamond in the sty."

When elected president of the Society of British Artists, Whistler naturally felt exultant. "Carr," he said, jokingly, to Conryns Carr, the dramatist, "you haven't congratulated me yet."

"No," was the retort. "I'm waiting till the correspondence begins!"

* * * * *

The Society did not possess a Royal Charter until Mr. Whistler became president. With some help from the Prince of Wales this was procured. When the Prince paid his first visit to the gallery, Whistler was there to welcome him.

"I'm sure," said the Prince at the door, "I never heard of this place, Mr. Whistler, until you brought it to my notice. What is its history?"

"It has none, your Highness," was the neat rejoinder. "Its history dates from to-day!"

When Whistler left the White House, at Chelsea, he put this legend over the door:

"'Unless the Lord build the house, their labor is but vain that build it.' E.W. Godwin, P.S.A., built this one."

* * * * *

Justin McCarthy, the journalist and historian of **Our Own Times**, stayed away from the Whistler dinner at the Criterion because his friend Mortimer Menpes had been slighted. He met Whistler a few evenings later at a dinner to Christie Murray. As they came together Whistler remarked darkly:

"You're a bold man and a philanthropist; but remember, **Damien died**!"

And he had, just before, among the lepers of Molokai! Rather rough on the claimant of Lemon Yellow!

* * * * *

The Fine Art Society once billed Whistler for incidentals to one of his exhibitions, and thoughtfully included a pair of stockings worn by an attendant named Cox.

"I shall pay for nothing of Cox's," said the artist, indignantly. "Neither his socks, nor his 'ose, nor anything that is his."

* * * * *

One of his proofs, sold by Sotheby's in 1888--that of an early etching--brought a good price, not on its merits, but for this line by the artist, written on the margin: "Legs not by me, but a fatuous addition by a general practitioner."

The "legs" were by Dr. Seymour Haden, Whistler's eminent brother-in-law.

* * * * *

The eccentric relationship between Whistler and that self-destroyed genius, Oscar Wilde, has been much portrayed. A characteristic meeting was thus described by a correspondent of the London *Literary World*:

"Whistler and Wilde were to be the lions at a literary reception. Unfortunately, the lions came too early, when the few previous arrivals were altogether too insignificant to be introduced to them. So they had to talk to each other. It was on a very warm Sunday afternoon in the season, and Whistler, by the by, was wearing a white 'duck' waistcoat and trousers, and a fabulously long frock-coat, made, I think, of black alpaca, and carrying a brass-tipped stick about four feet long in his right hand, and a wonderful new paint-box, of which he was proud, under his left arm. Neither of the lions took any notice of what the other said. Finally, Wilde, who had spent the previous summer in America, began: 'Jimmy, this time last year, when I was in New York, all we men were carrying fans. It should be done here.' Instead of replying, Whistler observed that he had just returned from Paris, and that he always came by the Dieppe route, because it gave you so much longer for painting sea effects. Whether Oscar thought he was going to have an opportunity of scoring or what, he was tempted to break through the contempt with which-he had treated Whistler's other remarks. 'And how many did you paint in four hours, Jimmy?' he asked, with his most magnificent air of patronage. 'I'm not sure,' said the irrepressible Jimmy, quite gravely, 'but I think four or five hundred.'"

* * * * *

A London visitor at the Lambs Club recounted a new version of the notable enmity which followed the friendship that had existed between Whistler and Wilde. The latter one day asked the artist's opinion upon a poem which he had written, presenting a copy to be read. Whistler read it and was handing it back without comment.

"Well," queried Wilde, "do you perceive any worth?"

"It's worth its weight in gold," replied Whistler.

The poem was written on the very thinnest tissue-paper, weighing practically nothing. The coolness between the two men is said to have dated from that moment.

* * * * *

Walking up to Du Maurier and Wilde at the time the former was portraying the Postlethwaites in *Punch*, Whistler asked, whimsically, "I say, which of you invented the other, eh?"

* * * * *

When Oscar Wilde was married, this Whistler telegram met him at the door of St. James's Church, Sussex Gardens:

"Fear I may not be able to reach you in time for ceremony--don't wait."

* * * * *

"Heaven!" said Oscar once, when the two were together at Forbes-Robertson's and a pert flash fell from the artist's lips. "I wish I had said that!"

"Never mind, dear Oscar--you will," retorted Whistler.

* * * * *

When Lady Archibald Campbell sat for her portrait Lord Archibald was quite uncomfortable at the idea, and made certain that it was a condescension, not a commission. The painting was duly completed, received its due of scathing criticism, and became famous. At this the lady, meeting the artist, remarked:

"I hear my portrait has been exhibited everywhere and become famous."

"Sh-sh-sh!" he said. "So it has, my dear Lady Archibald, but every discretion has been exercised that Lord Archibald could desire. Your name is not mentioned. The portrait is known as 'The Yellow Buckskin.'"

* * * * *

Carlyle told Whistler he liked his portrait because the painter had given him "clean linen." Watts had made his collar green in a previous portrait.

* * * * *

Sitting wearied Carlyle. One day as he left the studio he met little Miss Alexander tripping in for her turn, and asked her name.

"I am Miss Alexander," she said, "and I am going to have my portrait painted."

"Puir lassie, puir lassie," murmured the old philosopher, pityingly.

* * * * *

Whistler's interest was aroused when the Cyclopeans were building the Savoy Hotel. "Hurry!" he said. "Where are my things? I must catch that now, for it will never again be so beautiful."

* * * * *

His model once asked him:
"Where were you born?"
"I never was born, my child; I came from on high."
The model retorted:
"Now that shows how easily we deceive ourselves in this world, for I should say you came from below!"

* * * * *

Invited once to dine with some eminences, the dinner-hour found him busy with his brush and engrossed in his subject. A friend who was to accompany him to the feast urged that it was frightfully late. "Don't you think you had better stop?" he asked.

"Stop?" shrieked Whistler. "Stop when everything is going so beautifully? Go and stuff myself with food when I can paint like this? Never! Never! Besides, they won't do anything until I get there. They never do."

* * * * *

Whistler was in a London shop one day when a customer came in who mistook him for a clerk.

"I say, this 'at doesn't fit!"

"Neither does your coat," observed the painter, after eying him critically.

* * * * *

A young woman student protested under criticism, "Mr. Whistler, is there any reason why I shouldn't paint things as I see them?"

"Well, really, there is no statute against it; but the dreadful moment will be when you see things as you painted them!"

"Britain's Realm," by John Brett, R.A., now in the National Gallery at Millbank, made a stir when first exhibited at the Academy. It shows the sea. Whistler walked into a wave of adulation one day during the exhibition, and, affecting to "knock" with his knuckles, said sardonically: "Ha! Ha! Tin! If you threw a stone on to this it would make a rumbling noise!"

* * * * *

His early price for the use of one of his lithographs by a magazine was ten guineas. Later he charged twenty, either sum being petty enough. To one editor who tendered ten pounds he wrote:

"Guineas, M. le Rédacteur; guineas, not pounds!"

* * * * *

At a reception one evening in Prince's Hall he was introduced to Henrietta Rae, whose painting "Psyche Before the Throne of Venus" had made her notable. She had been described to him in advance as rather weighty in figure.

"I don't think you're a bit too fat," was his encouraging greeting.

* * * * *

"Why have you withered people and stung them all your life?" asked a lady.

"My dear," he said, "I will tell you a secret. Early in life I made the discovery that I was charming; and if one is delightful, one has to thrust the world away to keep from being bored to death."

* * * * *

During the Boxer troubles, when Pekin was under siege to rescue the legations, he remarked:

"Dear! dear! I hope they will save the palace. All the Englishmen in the world are not worth one blue china vase."

One evening at Pennell's Miss Annulet Andrews mentioned attending the Royal Society soirée the evening before.

"Poor thing!" he said. "Poor, misguided child! Did you come all the way to London to consort with such--well, what shall we call them? Why, there isn't a fellow among them who had his h's five years ago!"

* * * * *

"You should be grateful to me," said Whistler to Leyland, after he had painted the Peacock Room in the latter's house. "I have made you famous. My work will live when you are forgotten. Still, perchance in the dim ages to come you may be remembered as the proprietor of the Peacock Room."

* * * * *

Whistler's butterfly was the moth of the silkworm borrowed from Hokusai. Otto H. Bacher thought the addition of a sting to the signature came from this incident at Venice: In 1880 he found a scorpion and impaled it on his etching needle. As the little creature writhed and struck, Whistler exclaimed: "Look at the beggar now! See him strike! Isn't he fine? Look at him! Look at him now! See how hard he hits! That's right--that's the way! Hit hard! And do you see the poison that comes out when he strikes? Isn't he superb?"

* * * * *

Referring long after to his retirement from West Point, where he had been a cadet for three years, the artist explained his fall by saying: "If silicon had been a gas, I should have been a soldier!"

* * * * *

He was always proud of his West Point cadetship. "West Point is America," he would say. Julian Alden Weir, son of Whistler's instructor at the Academy, once dining with him in London, chanced to remark that football had been introduced at the school. "Good God!" cried Whistler. "A West Point cadet to be rolled in the mud by a Harvard junior!"

* * * * *

When a student at the Point he had the habit of combing his long hair in class with his fingers, which brought this frequent command from Lieutenant Caleb Huse:

"Mr. Whistler, go to your room and comb your hair!"

* * * * *

Examined on history at West Point, he failed to recall the date of the battle of Buena Vista. "Suppose," said the exasperated instructor, "you were to go out to dinner and the company began to talk of the Mexican War, and you, a West Point man, were asked the date of the battle; what would you do?"

"Do?" was the reply. "Why, I should refuse to associate with people who could talk of such things at dinner!"

* * * * *

He disliked the work of the riding class at West Point, and one day wished to exchange his heavy horse for a lighter animal. The dragoon in charge called out: "Oh, don't swap, don't you swap! Yours is a war-horse!"

"A war-horse!" exclaimed the little cadet. "That settles it. I certainly don't want him!"

"Yes, you do, sir," insisted the dragoon. "He's a war-horse, I tell you, for he'd rather die than run!"

* * * * *

"Of course you don't know what fear is," observed Mortimer Menpes.

"Ah, yes, I do!" Whistler answered. "I should hate, for example, to be standing opposite a man who was a better shot than I, far away out in the forest, in the bleak, cold, early morning. Fancy me, the master, standing out in the open as a target to be shot at. Pshaw! It would be foolish and inartistic. I never mind calling a man out; but I always have the sense to know he is not likely to come."

* * * * *

Mr. Howard Mansfield relates that while in London in the summer of 1900 with Mr. Whistler, reference was one day made to West Point. He broke at once into enthusiastic praise of that institution, declaring that there was no finer institution in the world, and adding that next to it came the Naval Academy at Annapolis. Then he went on to say: "What was it which really saved you in your late deplorable war with the politest nation of Europe but the bearing of your naval gentlemen? After the affair in that sea--what's its name?--off the island of Cuba, when dear old Admiral Cervera was fished up like a dollop of cotton out of an ink-pot and was received on one of your ships with all the honors due to his rank, the officers all saluting and the crew manning the yards, as it were--only they haven't any yards now--but lined up in quite the proper way--why, it was splendid, just splendid!"

* * * * *

Dining one night at a house where there were a number of his pictures about the room, he could give attention to nothing but his own work. When he left he begged that one painting be sent to his studio to be revarnished. The unsuspecting hostess complied. Once delivered, she could not get it back. Finally she wrote: "I can live no longer without my beautiful picture, and I am sending to have it taken away."

"Isn't it appalling?" he cried to Menpes. "Just think of it! Ten years ago this woman bought my picture for a ridiculously small sum, a mere bagatelle, a few pounds; she has had the privilege of living with this masterpiece for ten whole years, and now she has the presumption to ask for it back again. Pshaw! The thing's unspeakable!"

* * * * *

"What a series of accidents!" was his comment on a row of Turners at the National Gallery.

* * * * *

On another occasion, when he arrived at his host's house two hours after the time set for dining, he found the meal well under way. "How extraordinary!" he exclaimed to the amazed company.

"Really, I should think you could have waited a bit. Why, you're just like a lot of pigs with your eating!"

* * * * *

Sir John E. Millais said to Whistler one day: "Jimmy, why don't you paint more pictures? Put out more canvases!"

"I know better," was the shrewd reply. "The fool!" he muttered, as he entered his studio. "He spreads himself on canvas on every possible occasion, and, do you know, he called me Jimmy! Mind you, I don't know the fellow well at all."

* * * * *

His "Nocturne in Blue and Gold, Valparaiso," was in the Hill collection at Brighton. Whistler made Mr. Hill a visit which he thus described: "I was shown into the galleries, and, of course, took a chair and sat looking at my beautiful 'Nocturne'; then, as there was nothing else to do, I went to sleep."

In this state Mr. Hill found him!

This sleeping habit was common with him when the company or the goings-on failed to interest him. On one occasion his sweet snore alarmed his neighbor, who nudged him and whispered:

"I say, Whistler, you must not sleep here!"

"Leave me alone!" commanded the artist, crossly. "I've said all I wanted to. I've no interest at all in what you and your friends have to say."

* * * * *

He once slumbered through a dinner where Edwin A. Abbey was a fellow-guest. The next morning he blandly asked Mr. Chase:

"What did Abbey have to say last night? Anything worth while?"

When Dan Smith was at the beginning of his career as an illustrator he was employed by an important lithographing house. One day, while making a large picture of Antony and Cleopatra in the barge scene, which was to be used by Kyrle Bellew and Mrs. James Brown Potter as a poster for their joint starring tour, Whistler, accompanied by a friend, visited the studio:

Whistler examined, with evident interest and approval, the canvas upon which the youthful artist was at work, holding his glass to his eyes; then, looking quizzically over it, remarked to his friend, "What a mercantile wretch it is!"

* * * * *

Whistler presented a copy of his edition of ***The Gentle Art of Making Enemies*** to "Theodore Watts, the Worldling."

Asked why he started the unlucky school in the Latin Quarter, he answered:

"It was for Carmen Rossi [long his model], poor little Carmen, who is a mere child and has no money, and is saddled with the usual Italian burden of a large, disreputable family--banditti brothers, a trifling husband, and all the rest of it."

"Carmen" was then thirty years old; weight, one hundred and ninety pounds. But she once had been his child-model.

* * * * *

A Scotch student in the class had worked out the face of an old peasant woman illuminated by a candle. "How beautifully you have painted the candle!" Whistler commended. "Good morning, gentlemen!"

* * * * *

One day, when the pupils had been sketching from life, he came upon the work of one which, if it contained all of the truth, did not contain all of the beautiful.

After gazing at it for some time Whistler observed to the student:

"Ah, well! You can hardly expect me to teach you morals." And he walked away.

* * * * *

A carelessly kept palette was an abhorrence to the painter. He would inspect those used by his class, and on the discovery of untidiness uttered a reproof like this: "My friends, have you noticed the way in which a musician cares for his violin? How beautiful it is? How well kept? How tenderly handled? Your palette is your instrument, its colors the notes, and upon it you play your symphonies!"

* * * * *

The colloquies with the class were spirited, sarcastic, interesting. Here is a characteristic one:

Question: "Do you know what I mean when I say tone, value, light, shade, quality, movement, construction, etc.?"

Chorus: "Oh, yes, Mr. Whistler!"

Mr. Whistler: "I'm glad, for it's more than I do myself!"

* * * * *

He objected to smoking in the atelier, partly because it obscured the light and partly because of its obfuscating qualities. In Paris a big Englishman clouded the class-room with a copious discharge of smoke. "My dear sir," said Whistler, gently, "I know you do not smoke to show disrespect for my request that students refrain from smoking on the days I come to them, nor would you desire to infringe upon the rules of the atelier, but--er--it seems to me--er--that when you are painting--er--you might possibly become so absorbed in your work as to--er--let your cigar go out!"

Visiting Earl Stetson Crawford in his studio at Paris, he noted on the wall a photographic copy of the Nicholson portrait of himself.

"Is that the best you have of me?" he asked. "Not that it is not very beautiful and artistic and so on--but I say, come now, you don't think it quite does me justice, do you?"

* * * * *

When the class was formed, so runs the tale, Whistler inquired of each pupil with whom he had studied before.
"With Julian," said one.
"Couldn't have done better, sir," Whistler answered.
"With Chase," replied another.
"Couldn't have done better, sir."
"With Mowbray," answered a third.
"Couldn't have done better, sir," and so on.
He approached a student slightly deaf, who stammered in reply, "I beg pardon?"
"Couldn't have done better, sir," responded Whistler, placidly, passing on to the next.

* * * * *

"It suffices not, Messieurs," he once observed to the class, "that a life spent among pictures makes a painter, else the policeman in the National Gallery might assert himself."

* * * * *

A pupil told him proudly she had studied with Bouguereau.
"Bouguereau! Bouguereau! Who is Bouguereau?"

* * * * *

One young lady in the class offended him. She received a polite note, signed with a neat butterfly, requesting her not to attend further. "It was worth being expelled to get the note," she said. Whistler heard of the comment.

"Well, they'll all have a note some day," he observed. His retirement soon followed.

* * * * *

H. Villiers Barnett, editor of the **Continental Weekly**, when in the employ of the *Magazine of Art* visited the Dowdeswell Gallery at a press view of the Venice pastels. He alone of the critics developed some interest, and soon found himself alone with Whistler.

"I beg your pardon," said the latter, "but do you represent a religious journal?"

"No," Barnett replied, jokingly, "mine is an out-and-out sporting paper!"

"Oh," said Whistler, "that accounts for it."

"Accounts for what?"

"Well, you see," said Whistler, with an exquisite sneer, "I have been watching you gentlemen of the press all morning. You are the only one in the whole lot who seems to find anything here worth looking at, and you have been taking such very serious interest that I was certain you must be representing some church paper."

"Mr. Whistler," retorted Barnett, "make your mind easy. There is nothing ecclesiastical about me nor the publication I have the honor to represent; but all the same, for you this is the day of judgment!"

"I wish you good morning," rejoined the painter, pertly.

* * * * *

His "artistic" make-up of flat-brimmed hat, lemon-colored vest, curls, eyeglass, and beribboned cane sometimes upset the cockney crowd. R.A.M. Stevenson, cousin of Robert Louis, was working in his studio one day when the bell rang violently. He ran to the door just in time to rescue the symphony into which Whistler had turned himself from a growling mob.

"For God's sake, Stevenson," said Whistler, "save me from these howling brutes!"

He went home in a cab with all his trimmings.

* * * * *

Harper Pennington has revealed to us the origin of the "standing-room only" joke. It appears that there was hardly ever any furniture in Whistler's house. He was peculiarly parsimonious in the matter of chairs. This led to a remark of Corny Grain's which became famous.

"Ah, Jimmy! Glad to see you playing to such a full house!" said Dick (Corny) Grain when shaking hands before a Sunday luncheon, while glaring around the studio with his large, protruding eyes, in search of something to sit on.

"What do you mean?" asked Whistler.

"Standing-room only," replied the actor.

* * * * *

Henry Labouchere, who first met Whistler as a boy in Washington in the fifties, when he himself was an attaché of the British Legation, took the credit for bringing Whistler and his wife together. His story was denied by Mrs. Whistler's relatives, but is interesting enough to be recorded.

"I believe," wrote Mr. Labouchere in *Truth*, "I was responsible for his marriage to the widow of Mr. Godwin, the architect. She was a remarkably pretty woman and very agreeable, and both she and he were thorough Bohemians.

"I was dining with them and some others one evening at Earl's Court. They were obviously greatly attracted to each other, and in a vague sort of way they thought of marrying, so I took the matter in hand to bring things to a practical point.

"'Jimmy,' I said, 'will you marry Mrs. Godwin?'

"'Certainly.'

"'Mrs. Godwin,' I said, 'will you marry Jimmy?'

"'Certainly,' she replied.

"'When?' I asked.

"'Oh, some day,' said Whistler.

"'That won't do,' I said. 'We must have a date.'

"So they both agreed that I should choose the day, tell them what church to come to for the ceremony, provide a clergyman, and give the bride away.

"I fixed an early date and got them the chaplain of the House of Commons to perform the ceremony. It took place a few days later. After the ceremony was over we adjourned to Whistler's studio, where he had prepared a banquet. The banquet was on the table, but there were no chairs, so we sat on packing-cases. The happy pair, when I left, had not quite decided whether they would go that evening to Paris or remain in the studio.

"How unpractical they were was shown when I happened to meet the bride the day before the marriage in the street.

"'Don't forget to-morrow,' I said.

"'No,' she replied; 'I am just going to buy my trousseau.'

"'A little late for that, is it not?' I asked.

"'No,' she answered, 'for I am only going to buy a tooth-brush and a new sponge, as one ought to have new ones when one marries.'

"However, there never was a more successful marriage. They adored each other, and lived most happily together, and when she died he was broken-hearted indeed. He never recovered from the loss."

* * * * *

When Frederick Keppel, the American print expert, first called upon the artist at the Tite Street studio, the famous portrait of Sarasate, "black on black," stood at the end of the long corridor that he used to form a vista for proper perspective of his work. Laying his hand on Keppel's shoulder, he said:

"Now, isn't it beautiful?"

"It certainly is," was the reply.

"No," said he; "but isn't it ***beautiful?***"

"It is indeed," said Keppel.

This was too mild a form of agreement. Whistler raised his voice to a scream:

"D---n it, man!" he piped. "Isn't it BEAUTIFUL?"

Adopting the emphasis and the exclamation, Mr. Keppel shouted:

"D----n it, it is!"

This was satisfactory.

* * * * *

The proof-sheets of ***The Gentle Art***, Whistler version, had just arrived as Mr. Keppel called. "Read them aloud," he commanded, "so I can hear how it sounds."

Mr. Keppel started in, but his elocution was not satisfactory.

"Stop!" Whistler cried. "You are murdering it! Let me read it to you!"

He read about two hours to his own keen delight, but was finally interrupted by a servant announcing, "Lady ----."

"Where is she?" asked the artist.

"In her carriage at the door."

He went on reading until Mr. Keppel suggested that he had forgotten the lady.

"Oh," he said, carelessly, "let her wait! I'm mobbed with these people."

After another quarter-hour he condescended to go down and greet her shivering ladyship.

* * * * *

A little later during this visit a foreign artist called and was pleasantly received. Admiring a small painting, the visitor said:

"Now, that is one of your good ones."

"Don't look at it, dear boy," replied Whistler, airily; "it's not finished."

"Finished!" said the visitor. "Why, it's the most carefully finished picture of yours I've seen."

"Don't look at it," insisted Whistler. "You are doing an injustice to yourself, you are doing an injustice to the picture, and you're doing an injustice to me!"

Then, theatrically:

"Stop! I'll finish it now." With that he picked a very small brush, anointed, its delicate point with paint, and touched the picture in one spot with a speck of pigment.

"Now it's finished!" he exclaimed. "Now you may look at it."

Forgetting his umbrella, the foreign gentleman called at the studio the next day to get it. Whistler was out, but the visitor was much moved to find the "finishing touch" had been carefully wiped off!

* * * * *

Mr. Keppel's personal relations with Whistler ended when, by an idle chance, he sent a copy of ***The University of the State of New York Bulletin, Bibliography, No. I, a Guide to the Study of James Abbott McNeill Whistler***, compiled by Walter Greenwood Forsyth and Joseph Le Roy Harrison, to Joseph Pennell, and another to Ernest Brown, in London. Mr. Keppel, arriving in London the day of Mrs. Whistler's funeral, sent a note of condolence, and, receiving a mourning envelope sealed with a black butterfly, opened it expecting a grateful acknowledgment. Instead, it was a fierce, rasping denunciation for the distribution of the pamphlet--a mere catalogue so far as it went.

"I must not let the occasion of your being in town pass," he wrote, "without acknowledging the gratuitous zeal with which you have done your best to further the circulation of one of the most malignant innuendos, in the way of scurrilous half-assertions, it has been my fate hitherto to meet. Mr. Brown very properly sent on to me the pamphlet you had promptly posted to him. Mr. Pennell, also, I find, you had carefully supplied with a copy--and I have no doubt that, with the untiring energy of the 'busy' one, you have smartly placed the pretty work in the hands of many another before this."

* * * * *

Mr. Keppel replied in kind, but Whistler never wrote him directly again. Some business letter of the former requiring a reply, he summoned the house-porter, who wrote under dictation, beginning his crude epistle thus: "Sir:--Mr. Whistler, who is present, orders me to write as follows." Roiled by this beyond measure, Mr. Keppel resorted to verse to relieve his feelings, after which Whistler twice sent verbal messages through friends that if he ever saw him again he would kill him!

* * * * *

John M. Cauldwell, the United States Commissioner for the Department of Art at the Paris Exposition of 1900, sent a circular letter to American artists in the city announcing his arrival and making appointments to discuss the hanging of their work. Whistler received one, asking him to call at "precisely four-thirty" on the afternoon of the following Thursday.

"I congratulate you," he replied. "Personally, I never have been able and never shall be able to be anywhere at precisely four-thirty."

* * * * *

"Parbleu! This is a nice get-up to come and see me in, to be sure!" was his greeting to a newspaper writer who called to tap him on art, clad in a brown jacket, blue trousers, and decked with a red necktie. "I must request you to leave this place instantly! These scribblers, rag-smudges, *incroyable*! Why, it is perfectly preposterous! Did you ever hear such dissonance? His tie is in G major, and I am painting this symphony in E minor. I will have to start it again. Take that roaring tie of yours off, you miserable wretch! Remove it instantly!"

The visitor removed the "roar." "Thank goodness!" said Whistler. "My sight is perfectly deaf!"

"I am so sorry, Mr. Whistler," apologized the scribe.

"Whistler, sir? Whistler? That's not my name!" he cried, in a highly wrought voice.

"I beg your pardon?"

"That is not my name. I say, you don't seem to know your own language. W-h is pronounced Wh-h-h--Wh-h-histler. Bah!"

* * * * *

Max Beerbohm, the caricaturist, was rather clumsy with the Gallic tongue. Whistler used to term it "Max Beerbohm's Limburger French."

The carefully cultivated and insistently displayed white lock played a part in many amusing incidents. Sir Coutts Lindsay's butler whispered to him excitedly one evening: "There's a gent downstairs says he's come to dinner, wot's forgot his necktie and stuck a feather in his 'air."

Another evening, at the theater, an usher said obligingly: "Beg pardon, sir, but there's a white feather in your hair, just on top."

* * * * *

Raging characteristically once when in Paris, he earned this rebuke from Degas, the matchless draughtsman: "Whistler, you talk as if you were a man without talent."

* * * * *

Some one gave Henry Irving a Whistler etching for a Christmas gift. "Of course I was delighted," he said, "for I was a great admirer of the artist as well as a personal friend of the man, but when I started to hang the etching I was puzzled. I couldn't for the life of me tell which was the top and which the bottom. Finally, after reversing the picture half a dozen times and finding it looked equally well either way up, I decided to try an experiment.

"I invited Whistler to dine with me and seated him opposite his picture. During dinner he glanced at it from time to time; between the soup and the fish he put up his eyeglass and squinted at it; between the roast and the dessert he got up and walked over to take a closer view of it; finally, by the time we reached the coffee, he had discovered what the trouble was.

"'Why, Henry,' he said, reproachfully, 'you've hung my etching upside down.'

"'Indeed!' I said. 'Well, my friend, it's taken you an hour to discover it!'" "The man in possession" furnishes an amusing incident in the artist's career.

When the creditors at last landed a bailiff in the painter's Chelsea mansion, he tried to wear his hat in the drawing-room and smoke and spit all over the house. But Whistler, in his own airy way, soon settled that. He went out into the hall, and, selecting a stick from his collection of canes, he daintily knocked the man's hat off. The bailiff was so surprised that he forgot to be angry, and in a day or two he had been trained to wait at table. But though he was now in possession and a favored household servant, he could not obtain his money. So he declared that if he was not paid he would have to put bills up outside the house announcing a sale. And sure enough, a few days after great posters were stuck up all over the front of the house announcing so many tables and so many chairs and so much old Nankin China for sale on a given day. Whistler enjoyed the joke hugely, and hastened to send out invitations to all his friends to a luncheon-party, adding as a postscript: "You will know the house by the bills of sale stuck up outside." And the bailiff proved an admirable butler and the party one of the merriest ever known.

As the guests were rising from the table a lady observed to the host:

"Your servants seem to be extremely attentive, Mr. Whistler, and anxious to please you."

"Oh, yes," replied he; "I assure you they wouldn't leave me!"

But the bailiff stayed on, and the day of sale approached; so Whistler, having been educated at West Point, determined to practise strategy. Some one had told him that a mixture of snuff and beer had the property of sending people off to sleep. So he bought a big parcel of snuff and put the greater part of it into a gigantic tankard of beer, which he sent out to the bailiff in the garden. It was a very hot summer afternoon, and the man eagerly welcomed his refreshment. Whistler was in his studio painting and soon forgot all about him. In the evening he said to his servant, "Where's the man?" The servant replied: "I don't know, sir. I suppose he must have gone away."

The next morning Whistler got up very late and went out into the garden, where he was astonished to see the bailiff sitting in precisely the same position as the day before. The empty tankard was on the table beside him and his pipe had fallen from his hand upon the grass. "Hello, my sleeping beauty!" said Whistler. "Have you been there all night?" But the man made no answer, and all the painter's efforts to rouse him were unavailing. Late in the afternoon, however, he awoke in the most natural way in the world, exclaiming that it was dreadfully hot weather and that he must have been asleep over an hour. Whistler's strategy had been even more successful than he anticipated; the bailiff had slept through the entire day appointed for the sale of the painter's household effects, and was induced to go away in a very bewildered state of mind and with a small payment on account in his pocket.

* * * * *

Lady de Grey went once to the Tite Street studio for luncheon and chided Whistler for his extravagance in having two man servants to wait on the table, when he was always complaining of being hard up.

"Hush!" whispered Whistler. "One of them is the man in possession, and he has consented to act as footman for the day; but he asks me to please settle up as soon as possible, because he too has a man in possession at his own place and wants to get clear of him."

* * * * *

Once at a garden party the rapt hostess rushed up to the artist and exclaimed:

"Oh, Mr. Whistler! Do help me out! I have just bought a magnificent Turner, but Lord----says it isn't genuine, merely a clever imitation. Now I want you to look at it, and if you say it is genuine, as I know you will, I shall be perfectly satisfied."

"My dear lady," replied Whistler, "you expect a good deal of me. The distinction between a real Turner and an imitation Turner is so extremely subtle."

* * * * *

A flippant reply to the secretary of a London club where Whistler's account was past due produced this retort--and the money was paid:

"DEAR MR. WHISTLER:--It is not a Nocturne in Purple or a Symphony in Blue and Gray we are after, but an Arrangement in Gold and Silver."

* * * * *

At an exhibition at the Academy of Fine Arts there was a portrait in subdued colors by Whistler, "The Little Lady of Soho." Before this picture Secretary Harrison S. Morris stood one day. "It is beautiful," he observed, "and it reminds me of a story about Whistler--not a very appropriate or poetical one, perhaps. But here it is, anyhow. Whistler one summer day took a walk through the Downs with three or four young men. They stopped at an ale-house and called for beer. Tankards were set before them and they drank. Then Whistler said to the host:

"'My man, would you like to sell a great deal more beer than you do?'

"'Aye, sir, I would that!'

"'Then don't sell so much froth!'"

* * * * *

When a French magazine located his birthplace in Baltimore, and the error traveled far, Whistler took no pains to correct it. "My dear cousin Kate," he said to Mrs. Livermore, "if any one likes to think I was born in Baltimore, why should I deny it? It is of no consequence to me."

* * * * *

A chance American introduced himself by saying: "You know, Mr. Whistler, we were born at Lowell, and at very much the same time. You are sixty-seven and I am sixty-eight."

"Very charming," he replied. "And so you are sixty-eight and were born at Lowell. Most interesting, no doubt, and as you please! But I shall be born when and where I want, and I do not choose to be born in Lowell and I refuse to be sixty-seven!"

* * * * *

"Don't be afraid," said Whistler to Howard Paul, who recoiled from the presence of a huge dog because he did not like the look in the animal's eyes. "Look at his tail--how it wags. When a dog wags his tail he's in good humor."

"That may be," replied Paul, "but observe the wild glitter in his eye! I don't know which end to believe."

* * * * *

Comyns Carr met a foreign painter who had been known to breakfast with Whistler at Chelsea and asked him if he had seen him lately.

"Ah no, not now so much," was the reply. "He ask me a little while ago to breakfast, and I go. My cab-fare two shilling, 'arf crown. I arrive. Very nice. Goldfish in bowl. Very pretty. But breakfast! One egg, one toast, no more! Ah, no! My cab-fare back, two shilling, 'arf crown. For me no more!"

* * * * *

A.G. Plowden, the London police magistrate, attended a private view at Grosvenor Gallery. The first person he met was Whistler. He took Plowden, very amiably, to his full-length portrait of Lady Archibald Campbell, where, after sufficiently expressing his admiration, Plowden asked if there were any other pictures he ought to see.

"Other pictures!" cried Whistler, in a tone of horror. "Other pictures! There are no other pictures! You are through!"

* * * * *

Dining at a Paris restaurant in his early days, Mr. Whistler noted the struggle an elderly Englishman was having to make himself understood. He politely volunteered to interpret.

"Sir," said the person addressed, "I assure you, sir, I can give my order without assistance!"

"Can you indeed?" quoth Whistler, airily. "I fancied the contrary just now, when I heard you desire the waiter to bring you a pair of stairs."

* * * * *

Dining, and dining well, at George H. Boughton's house in London, Whistler was obliged to leave the table and go up-stairs to indite a note. In a few moments a great noise revealed the fact that he had fallen down the flight.

"Who is your architect?" he asked, when picked up.

The host told him Norman Shaw.

"I might have known it," said Whistler. "The d----d teetotaler!"

* * * * *

A young artist had brought Whistler to view his maiden effort. The two stood before the canvas for some moments in silence. Finally the junior asked, timidly:

"Don't you think this painting of mine is a--er--a tolerable picture, sir?"

Whistler's eyes twinkled.

"What is your opinion of a tolerable egg?" he asked.

* * * * *

"Irish girls have the most beautiful hands," he once wrote, "with long, slender fingers and delightful articulations. American girls' hands come next; they are a little narrow and thin. The hands of the English girls are red and coarse. The German hand is broad and flat; the Spanish hand is full of big veins. I always use Irish models for the hands, and I think Irish eyes are also the most beautiful."

An American artist studying in Paris, like many others, was too poor to have a perfect wardrobe. Strolling on the Boulevard, he heard a call and, turning, saw Whistler hastening toward him, waving his long black cane.

Rather flattered, he said, "So you recognized me from behind, did you, master?"

"Yes," said Whistler, with a wicked laugh; "I spied you through a hole in your coat."

* * * * *

"Do you think genius is hereditary?" asked an admiring lady one day.

"I can't tell you, madam," Whistler replied. "Heaven has granted me no offspring."

* * * * *

Whistler once took Horne, his framer, to look at one of his paintings at the exhibition.

"Well, Horne," he asked, "what do you think of it?"

"Think of it?" he cried, enthusiastically. "Why, sir, it's perfect--perfect. Mr. ---- has got one just like it."

"What!" said the puzzled Whistler. "A picture like this?"

"Oh," said Horne, "I wasn't talking about the picture; I was talking about the frame."

* * * * *

"Well, Mr. Whistler, how are you getting on?" said an undesirable acquaintance in a Paris restaurant.

"I'm not," said Whistler, emptying his glass. "I'm getting off."

* * * * *

Miss Pamela Smith, a designer in black and white, while a crude draughtsman, had a fine imagination. Whistler was asked to look over some of her work. After careful examination he said:

"She can't draw."

Another look and a gruff "She can't paint" followed.

A third look and a long thought wound up with, "But she doesn't need to."

* * * * *

A lady who rejoiced in "temperament" once said gushingly to Whistler:

"It is wonderful what a difference there is between people."

"Yes," he replied. "There is a great deal of difference between matches, too, if you will only look closely enough, but they all make about the same blaze."

* * * * *

A certain gentleman whose portrait Whistler had painted failed to appreciate the work, and finally remarked, "After all, Mr. Whistler, you can't call that a great work of art."

"Perhaps not," replied the painter, "but then you can't call yourself a great work of nature!"

* * * * *

The artist and a friend strolled along the Thames Embankment one wonderfully starry night. Whistler was in a discontented mood and found fault with everything. The houses were ugly, the river not what it might have been, the lights hard and glaring. The friend pointed out several things that appealed to him as beautiful, but the master would not give in.

"No," he said, "nature is only sometimes beautiful--only sometimes--very, very seldom indeed; and to-night she is, as so often, positively ugly."

"But the stars! Surely they are fine to-night," urged the other.

Whistler looked up at the sky.

"Yes," he drawled, "they're not bad, perhaps, but, my dear fellow, there's too many of them."

A sitter asked him how it was possible to paint in the growing dusk, as he often did. The reply was:

"As the light fades and the shadows deepen, all the petty and exacting details vanish; everything trivial disappears, and I see things as they are, in great, strong masses; the buttons are lost, but the garment remains; the garment is lost, but the sitter remains; the sitter is lost, but the shadow remains; the shadow is lost, but the picture remains. And that, night cannot efface from the painter's imagination."

* * * * *

Sir Laurence Alma-Tadema, of the classic brush, loved yellow, a color which Whistler had annexed unto himself. Sir Laurence in employing the color in his decorations did not consider himself a plagiarist. He had not seen Whistler's. This defense led to a war of words. Whistler broke out:

"Sly Alma! His Romano-Dutch St. John's wooden eye has never looked upon them, and the fine jaundice of his flesh is none of the jaundice of my yellows. To-de-ma-boom-de-ay!"

* * * * *

Seated in a stall at the West End Theater one evening, he was constantly irritated by his next neighbor--a lady--who not only went out between the acts, but several times while the curtain was up. The space between the run of seats was narrow, and the annoyance as she squeezed past was considerable.

"Madam," he said at last, "I trust I do not incommode you by keeping my seat!"

* * * * *

He regarded the United States tariff on art as barbarous.

"When are you coming to America?" he was asked.

"When the tariff on art is removed."

The Copley Society asked his aid in making up their exhibition in Boston. He refused, saying:

"God bless me! Why should you hold an exhibition of pictures in America? The people do not care for art!"

"How do you know? You have not been there for many years."

"How do I know? Why, haven't you a law to keep out pictures and statues? Is it not in black and white that the works of the great masters must not enter America, that they are not wanted? A people that tolerate such a law have no love for art; their protestation is mere pretense."

* * * * *

Asked by a lady if a certain picture in a gallery was not indecent, he replied:
"No, madam. But your question is!"

Mark Twain visited the studio and, assuming an air of hopeless stupidity, approached a nearly completed painting and said:

"Not at all bad, Mr. Whistler; not at all bad. Only here in this corner," he added, reflectively, with a motion as if to rub out a cloud effect, "if I were you I'd do away with that cloud!"

"Gad, sir!" cried the painter. "Do be careful there! Don't you see the paint is not yet dry?"

"Oh, don't mind that," said Mark, sweetly. "I am wearing gloves, you see!"

They got on after that.

* * * * *

In Paris, Whistler and an English painter got into a turbulent talk over Velasquez at a studio tea. In the course of the argument Whistler praised himself extravagantly.

"It's a good thing we can't see ourselves as others see us," sneered the Briton.

"Isn't it, though?" rejoined Whistler, gently. "I know in my case I should grow intolerably conceited."

* * * * *

Financial necessities once caused the sale of Whistler's choice furnishings. Some of the family, returning to the house during his absence, found the floor covered with chalk diagrams, the largest of which was labeled: "This is the dining-table."

Surrounding it were a number of small squares, each marked: "This is a chair." Another square: "This is the sideboard."

* * * * *

Cope Whitehouse once described a boat-load of Egyptians "floating down the Nile with the thermometer one hundred and twenty degrees in the shade, and no shade."

"And no thermometer," interjected Whistler.

* * * * *

A lady sitter brought a cat with her and placed it on her knee. The cat was nervous and yowled continuously.

"Madam," said the vexed artist, "will you have the cat in the foreground or in the back yard?"

* * * * *

While painting one of his famous nocturnes a critic of considerable pretensions called. "Good heavens, Whistler!" he cried, "what in the world are you splashing at?"

"I am teaching art to posterity," Whistler replied, quietly.

"Oh!" said the critic, visibly relieved. "I was afraid you were painting for the Royal Academy."

"Oh, no," answered Whistler; "they do not want masterpieces there, but some of their picture-frames are exquisite and really worth bus-fare to look at."

* * * * *

Walking in the Champs-Elysées in Paris one morning, Whistler heard one Englishman say to another:

"See that chap over there?"

"What? That chap with the long hair and spindle legs?"

"Yes, that's the one. That's Whistler, the American, who thinks he's the greatest painter on earth."

Walking up to the pair, Whistler held out his hand and said gravely to the last speaker:

"Sir, I beg your acceptance of these ten centimes. Go buy yourself a little hay!"

* * * * *

Sitting for a portrait was an ordeal. Many were quite upset after a siege in the studio. One man annoyed the artist by saying at each dismissal:

"How-about that ear, Mr. Whistler? Don't forget to finish that." At the last session, all being finished but this ear, Whistler said, "Well, I think I'm through; now I'll sign it." This he did in a very solemn and important way.

"But my ear!" exclaimed the victim. "You're not going to leave it that way?"

"Oh," said Whistler, grimly, "you can put it in after you get home."

* * * * *

He occasionally contemplated visiting America in his late years, but the dread of the journey was too much for him to overcome. "If I escape the Atlantic," he said, "I shall be wrecked by some reporter at the pier." Finally, he definitely canceled his last proposed trip, observing airily: "One cannot continuously disappoint a continent."

"America," he once said, lightly, "is a country where I never can be a prophet."

* * * * *

Sir Rennell Rodd recalled that at a breakfast Waldo Story gave at Dieu-donné's in Paris there was a great company, including Whistler. Every one there was by the way of having written a book or painted a picture, or having in some way outraged the Philistine, with the exception of one young gentleman whose raison d'être was not so apparent as his high collar and the glory of his attire. He nevertheless intruded boldly into the talk and laid down his opinions very flatly. He even went so far as to combat some dictum of the master's, whereat that gentleman adjusted his glasses and, looking pleasantly at the youth, queried:

"And whose son are you?"

When Dorothy Menpes was a babe in the cradle a white feather lay across her infant brow. The sight pleased Whistler. "That child is going to develop into something great," he prophesied, "for see, she begins with a feather, just like me."

* * * * *

In the last two years of his life Mr. Whistler's disputes grew less frequent and his public flashes were few. The ***Morning Post*** of London, however, provoked an admirable specimen of his best style, which it printed under date of August 6th, 1902. In its "Art and Artists" column the paper had made the following statement:

"Mr. Whistler is so young in spirit that his friends must have read with surprise the Dutch physician's announcement that the present illness is due to 'advanced age.' In England sixty-seven is not exactly regarded as 'advanced age,' but even for the gay 'butterfly' time does not stand still, and some who are unacquainted with the details of Mr. Whistler's career, though they know his work well, will be surprised to learn that he was exhibiting at the Academy forty-three years ago. His contributions to the exhibition of 1859 were 'Two Etchings from Nature,' and at intervals during the following fourteen or fifteen years Mr. Whistler was represented at the Academy by a number of works, both paintings and etchings. In 1863 his contributions numbered seven in all, and in 1865 four. Among his Academy pictures of 1865 was the famous 'Little White Girl,' the painting that attracted so much attention at the Paris Exhibition of 1900. This picture--rejected at the Salon of 1863--was inspired, though the fact seems to have been forgotten of late, by the following lines of Swinburne:

> Come snow, come wind or thunder
> High up in air,
> I watch my face and wonder
> At my bright hair, etc."

Under date of August 3d Mr. Whistler sent from The Hague this brisk reply:

I feel it no indiscretion to speak of my "convalescence," since you have given it official existence.

May I, therefore, acknowledge the tender little glow of health induced by reading, as I sat here in the morning sun, the flattering attention paid me by your gentleman of the ready wreath and quick biography?

I cannot, as I look at my improving self with daily satisfaction, really believe it all--still it has helped to do me good!--and it is with almost sorrow that I must beg you, perhaps, to put back into its pigeonhole for later on this present summary and replace it with something preparatory, which, doubtless, you have also ready.

This will give you time, however, for some correction--if really it be worth while--but certainly the "Little White Girl," which was not rejected at the Salon of '63, was, I am forced to say, not "inspired by the following lines of Swinburne," for the one simple reason that those lines were only written, in my studio, after the picture was painted. And the writing of them was a rare and graceful tribute from the poet to the painter--a noble recognition of work by the production of a nobler one!

Again, of the many tales concerning the hanging at the Academy of the well-known portrait of the artist's mother, now at the Luxembourg, one is true--let us trust your gentleman may have time to find it out--that I may correct it. I surely may always hereafter rely on the ***Morning Post*** to see that no vulgar Woking joke reach me?

It is my marvelous privilege then to come back, as who should say, while the air is still warm with appreciation, affection, and regret, and to learn in how little I had offended. The continuing to wear my own hair and eyebrows, after distinguished confrères and eminent persons had long ceased their habit, has, I gather, clearly given pain. This, I see, is much remarked on. It is even found inconsiderate and unseemly in me, as hinting at affectation.

I might beg you, sir, to find a pretty place for this, that I would make my apology, containing also promise, in years to come, to lose these outer signs of vexing presumption.

Protesting, with full enjoyment of its unmerited eulogy, against your premature tablet, I ask you again to contradict it, and appeal to your own sense of kind sympathy when I tell you I learn that I have lurking in London still "a friend"--though for the life of me I cannot remember his name. And I have, sir, the honor to be,

J. MCNEILL WHISTLER.

The last dispute that found its way to print came through the New York *Sun* and Will H. Low, to whom Mr. Whistler sought to convey a piece of his mind *via* the newspaper channel, under date of May 8th, 1903, This grew out of a complication in which Mr. Low became involved with the Hanging Committee of the Society of American Artists over the placing in its exhibition of "Rosa Corder" and two marines by Whistler borrowed from Charles L. Freer, of Detroit, on the condition that they be hung "in a good position." The position selected did not suit Mr. Low, and he withdrew the pictures. Mr. Whistler sent his remonstrance to the *Sun's* London office, from which it was cabled to New York and published on May 9th, as follows:

"I had waited for Mr. Low to publish my reply to a letter from himself concerning the withdrawal of my pictures from the Society of American Artists.

"This gentle opinion of my own upon the situation is, I understand, expert. I therefore inclose it to you for publication. I have the honor to be, dear sir, your obedient servant."

The remarks to Mr. Low read:

"I have just learned with distress that my canvases have been a trouble and a cause of thought to the gentlemen of the Hanging Committee!

"Pray present to them my compliments and my deep regrets.

"I fear also that this is not the first time of simple and good-natured intrusion--looking in, as who would say, with beaming fellowship and crass camaraderie upon the highly finished table and well-seated guests--to be kindly and swiftly shuffled into some further respectable place--that all be well and hospitality endure.

"Promise, then, for me, that I have learned and that 'this shall not occur again.' And, above all, do not allow a matter of colossal importance to ever interfere with the afternoon habit of peace and good will, and the leaf of the mint so pleasantly associated with this society.

"I could not be other than much affected by your warm and immediate demonstration, but I should never forgive myself were the consequence of lasting vexation to your distinguished confrères."

www.bookjungle.com *email:* sales@bookjungle.com *fax:* 630-214-0564 *mail:* Book Jungle PO Box 2226 Champaign, IL 61825

The Codes Of Hammurabi And Moses
W. W. Davies

QTY

The discovery of the Hammurabi Code is one of the greatest achievements of archaeology, and is of paramount interest, not only to the student of the Bible, but also to all those interested in ancient history...

Religion **ISBN:** *1-59462-338-4* **Pages:** 132 *MSRP $12.95*

The Theory of Moral Sentiments
Adam Smith

QTY

This work from 1749. contains original theories of conscience amd moral judgment and it is the foundation for systemof morals.

Philosophy **ISBN:** *1-59462-777-0* **Pages:** 536 *MSRP $19.95*

Jessica's First Prayer
Hesba Stretton

QTY

In a screened and secluded corner of one of the many railway-bridges which span the streets of London there could be seen a few years ago, from five o'clock every morning until half past eight, a tidily set-out coffee-stall, consisting of a trestle and board, upon which stood two large tin cans, with a small fire of charcoal burning under each so as to keep the coffee boiling during the early hours of the morning when the work-people were thronging into the city on their way to their daily toil...

Childrens **ISBN:** *1-59462-373-2* **Pages:** 84 *MSRP $9.95*

My Life and Work
Henry Ford

QTY

Henry Ford revolutionized the world with his implementation of mass production for the Model T automobile. Gain valuable business insight into his life and work with his own auto-biography... "We have only started on our development of our country we have not as yet, with all our talk of wonderful progress, done more than scratch the surface. The progress has been wonderful enough but..."

Biographies/ **ISBN:** *1-59462-198-5* **Pages:** 300 *MSRP $21.95*

www.bookjungle.com email: sales@bookjungle.com fax: 630-214-0564 mail: Book Jungle PO Box 2226 Champaign, IL 61825

The Art of Cross-Examination
Francis Wellman

QTY

I presume it is the experience of every author, after his first book is published upon an important subject, to be almost overwhelmed with a wealth of ideas and illustrations which could readily have been included in his book, and which to his own mind, at least, seem to make a second edition inevitable. Such certainly was the case with me; and when the first edition had reached its sixth impression in five months, I rejoiced to learn that it seemed to my publishers that the book had met with a sufficiently favorable reception to justify a second and considerably enlarged edition. ..

Reference   ISBN: *1-59462-647-2*   Pages:412
MSRP *$19.95*

On the Duty of Civil Disobedience
Henry David Thoreau

QTY

Thoreau wrote his famous essay, On the Duty of Civil Disobedience, as a protest against an unjust but popular war and the immoral but popular institution of slave-owning. He did more than write—he declined to pay his taxes, and was hauled off to gaol in consequence. Who can say how much this refusal of his hastened the end of the war and of slavery?

Law   ISBN: *1-59462-747-9*   Pages:48
MSRP *$7.45*

Dream Psychology Psychoanalysis for Beginners
Sigmund Freud

QTY

Sigmund Freud, born Sigismund Schlomo Freud (May 6, 1856 - September 23, 1939), was a Jewish-Austrian neurologist and psychiatrist who co-founded the psychoanalytic school of psychology. Freud is best known for his theories of the unconscious mind, especially involving the mechanism of repression; his redefinition of sexual desire as mobile and directed towards a wide variety of objects; and his therapeutic techniques, especially his understanding of transference in the therapeutic relationship and the presumed value of dreams as sources of insight into unconscious desires.

Psychology   ISBN: *1-59462-905-6*   Pages:196
MSRP *$15.45*

The Miracle of Right Thought
Orison Swett Marden

QTY

Believe with all of your heart that you will do what you were made to do. When the mind has once formed the habit of holding cheerful, happy, prosperous pictures, it will not be easy to form the opposite habit. It does not matter how improbable or how far away this realization may see, or how dark the prospects may be, if we visualize them as best we can, as vividly as possible, hold tenaciously to them and vigorously struggle to attain them, they will gradually become actualized, realized in the life. But a desire, a longing without endeavor, a yearning abandoned or held indifferently will vanish without realization.

Self Help   ISBN: *1-59462-644-8*   Pages:360
MSRP *$25.45*

www.bookjungle.com email: sales@bookjungle.com fax: 630-214-0564 mail: Book Jungle PO Box 2226 Champaign, IL 61825

QTY

- [ ] **The Rosicrucian Cosmo-Conception Mystic Christianity** by *Max Heindel* ISBN: *1-59462-188-8* **$38.95**
The Rosicrucian Cosmo-conception is not dogmatic, neither does it appeal to any other authority than the reason of the student. It is: not controversial, but is: sent forth in the, hope that it may help to clear... *New Age/Religion Pages 646*

- [ ] **Abandonment To Divine Providence** by *Jean-Pierre de Caussade* ISBN: *1-59462-228-0* **$25.95**
"The Rev. Jean Pierre de Caussade was one of the most remarkable spiritual writers of the Society of Jesus in France in the 18th Century. His death took place at Toulouse in 1751. His works have gone through many editions and have been republished... *Inspirational/Religion Pages 400*

- [ ] **Mental Chemistry** by *Charles Haanel* ISBN: *1-59462-192-6* **$23.95**
Mental Chemistry allows the change of material conditions by combining and appropriately utilizing the power of the mind. Much like applied chemistry creates something new and unique out of careful combinations of chemicals the mastery of mental chemistry... *New Age Pages 354*

- [ ] **The Letters of Robert Browning and Elizabeth Barret Barrett 1845-1846 vol II** ISBN: *1-59462-193-4* **$35.95**
by *Robert Browning* and *Elizabeth Barrett* *Biographies Pages 596*

- [ ] **Gleanings In Genesis (volume I)** by *Arthur W. Pink* ISBN: *1-59462-130-6* **$27.45**
Appropriately has Genesis been termed "the seed plot of the Bible" for in it we have, in germ form, almost all of the great doctrines which are afterwards fully developed in the books of Scripture which follow... *Religion/Inspirational Pages 420*

- [ ] **The Master Key** by *L. W. de Laurence* ISBN: *1-59462-001-6* **$30.95**
In no branch of human knowledge has there been a more lively increase of the spirit of research during the past few years than in the study of Psychology, Concentration and Mental Discipline. The requests for authentic lessons in Thought Control, Mental Discipline and... *New Age/Business Pages 422*

- [ ] **The Lesser Key Of Solomon Goetia** by *L. W. de Laurence* ISBN: *1-59462-092-X* **$9.95**
This translation of the first book of the "Lernegton" which is now for the first time made accessible to students of Talismanic Magic was done, after careful collation and edition, from numerous Ancient Manuscripts in Hebrew, Latin, and French... *New Age/Occult Pages 92*

- [ ] **Rubaiyat Of Omar Khayyam** by *Edward Fitzgerald* ISBN: *1-59462-332-5* **$13.95**
Edward Fitzgerald, whom the world has already learned, in spite of his own efforts to remain within the shadow of anonymity, to look upon as one of the rarest poets of the century, was born at Bredfield, in Suffolk, on the 31st of March, 1809. He was the third son of John Purcell... *Music Pages 172*

- [ ] **Ancient Law** by *Henry Maine* ISBN: *1-59462-128-4* **$29.95**
The chief object of the following pages is to indicate some of the earliest ideas of mankind, as they are reflected in Ancient Law, and to point out the relation of those ideas to modern thought. *Religion/History Pages 452*

- [ ] **Far-Away Stories** by *William J. Locke* ISBN: *1-59462-129-2* **$19.45**
"Good wine needs no bush, but a collection of mixed vintages does. And this book is just such a collection. Some of the stories I do not want to remain buried for ever in the museum files of dead magazine-numbers an author's not unpardonable vanity..." *Fiction Pages 272*

- [ ] **Life of David Crockett** by *David Crockett* ISBN: *1-59462-250-7* **$27.45**
"Colonel David Crockett was one of the most remarkable men of the times in which he lived. Born in humble life, but gifted with a strong will, an indomitable courage, and unremitting perseverance... *Biographies/New Age Pages 424*

- [ ] **Lip-Reading** by *Edward Nitchie* ISBN: *1-59462-206-X* **$25.95**
Edward B. Nitchie, founder of the New York School for the Hard of Hearing, now the Nitchie School of Lip-Reading, Inc, wrote "LIP-READING Principles and Practice". The development and perfecting of this meritorious work on lip-reading was an undertaking... *How-to Pages 400*

- [ ] **A Handbook of Suggestive Therapeutics, Applied Hypnotism, Psychic Science** ISBN: *1-59462-214-0* **$24.95**
by *Henry Munro* *Health/New Age/Health/Self-help Pages 376*

- [ ] **A Doll's House: and Two Other Plays** by *Henrik Ibsen* ISBN: *1-59462-112-8* **$19.95**
Henrik Ibsen created this classic when in revolutionary 1848 Rome. Introducing some striking concepts in playwriting for the realist genre, this play has been studied the world over. *Fiction/Classics/Plays 308*

- [ ] **The Light of Asia** by *sir Edwin Arnold* ISBN: *1-59462-204-3* **$13.95**
In this poetic masterpiece, Edwin Arnold describes the life and teachings of Buddha. The man who was to become known as Buddha to the world was born as Prince Gautama of India but he rejected the worldly riches and abandoned the reigns of power when... *Religion/History/Biographies Pages 170*

- [ ] **The Complete Works of Guy de Maupassant** by *Guy de Maupassant* ISBN: *1-59462-157-8* **$16.95**
"For days and days, nights and nights, I had dreamed of that first kiss which was to consecrate our engagement, and I knew not on what spot I should put my lips..." *Fiction/Classics Pages 240*

- [ ] **The Art of Cross-Examination** by *Francis L. Wellman* ISBN: *1-59462-309-0* **$26.95**
Written by a renowned trial lawyer, Wellman imparts his experience and uses case studies to explain how to use psychology to extract desired information through questioning. *How-to/Science/Reference Pages 408*

- [ ] **Answered or Unanswered?** by *Louisa Vaughan* ISBN: *1-59462-248-5* **$10.95**
Miracles of Faith in China *Religion Pages 112*

- [ ] **The Edinburgh Lectures on Mental Science (1909)** by *Thomas* ISBN: *1-59462-008-3* **$11.95**
This book contains the substance of a course of lectures recently given by the writer in the Queen Street Hall, Edinburgh. Its purpose is to indicate the Natural Principles governing the relation between Mental Action and Material Conditions... *New Age/Psychology Pages 148*

- [ ] **Ayesha** by *H. Rider Haggard* ISBN: *1-59462-301-5* **$24.95**
Verily and indeed it is the unexpected that happens! Probably if there was one person upon the earth from whom the Editor of this, and of a certain previous history, did not expect to hear again... *Classics Pages 380*

- [ ] **Ayala's Angel** by *Anthony Trollope* ISBN: *1-59462-352-X* **$29.95**
The two girls were both pretty, but Lucy who was twenty-one who supposed to be simple and comparatively unattractive, whereas Ayala was credited, as her Bombwhat romantic name might show, with poetic charm and a taste for romance. Ayala when her father died was nineteen... *Fiction Pages 484*

- [ ] **The American Commonwealth** by *James Bryce* ISBN: *1-59462-286-8* **$34.45**
An interpretation of American democratic political theory. It examines political mechanics and society from the perspective of Scotsman James Bryce *Politics Pages 572*

- [ ] **Stories of the Pilgrims** by *Margaret P. Pumphrey* ISBN: *1-59462-116-0* **$17.95**
This book explores pilgrims religious oppression in England as well as their escape to Holland and eventual crossing to America on the Mayflower, and their early days in New England... *History Pages 268*

www.bookjungle.com email: sales@bookjungle.com fax: 630-214-0564 mail: Book Jungle PO Box 2226 Champaign, IL 61825

QTY

The Fasting Cure *by Sinclair Upton* ISBN: *1-59462-222-1* **$13.95**
In the Cosmopolitan Magazine for May, 1910, and in the Contemporary Review (London) for April, 1910, I published an article dealing with my experiences in fasting. I have written a great many magazine articles, but never one which attracted so much attention... *New Age/Self Help/Health Pages 164*

Hebrew Astrology *by Sepharial* ISBN: *1-59462-308-2* **$13.45**
In these days of advanced thinking it is a matter of common observation that we have left many of the old landmarks behind and that we are now pressing forward to greater heights and to a wider horizon than that which represented the mind-content of our progenitors... *Astrology Pages 144*

Thought Vibration or The Law of Attraction in the Thought World ISBN: *1-59462-127-6* **$12.95**
by William Walker Atkinson *Psychology/Religion Pages 144*

Optimism *by Helen Keller* ISBN: *1-59462-108-X* **$15.95**
Helen Keller was blind, deaf, and mute since 19 months old, yet famously learned how to overcome these handicaps, communicate with the world, and spread her lectures promoting optimism. An inspiring read for everyone... *Biographies/Inspirational Pages 84*

Sara Crewe *by Frances Burnett* ISBN: *1-59462-360-0* **$9.45**
In the first place, Miss Minchin lived in London. Her home was a large, dull, tall one, in a large, dull square, where all the houses were alike, and all the sparrows were alike, and where all the door-knockers made the same heavy sound... *Childrens/Classic Pages 88*

The Autobiography of Benjamin Franklin *by Benjamin Franklin* ISBN: *1-59462-135-7* **$24.95**
The Autobiography of Benjamin Franklin has probably been more extensively read than any other American historical work, and no other book of its kind has had such ups and downs of fortune. Franklin lived for many years in England, where he was agent... *Biographies/History Pages 332*

Name	
Email	
Telephone	
Address	
City, State ZIP	

☐ Credit Card   ☐ Check / Money Order

Credit Card Number	
Expiration Date	
Signature	

Please Mail to: Book Jungle
                   PO Box 2226
                   Champaign, IL 61825
or Fax to: 630-214-0564

ORDERING INFORMATION

web: *www.bookjungle.com*
email: *sales@bookjungle.com*
fax: *630-214-0564*
mail: *Book Jungle PO Box 2226 Champaign, IL 61825*
or PayPal *to sales@bookjungle.com*

Please contact us for bulk discounts

DIRECT-ORDER TERMS

**20% Discount if You Order
Two or More Books**
Free Domestic Shipping!
Accepted: Master Card, Visa,
Discover, American Express

www.ingramcontent.com/pod-product-compliance
Lightning Source LLC
Chambersburg PA
CBHW081327040426
42453CB00013B/2318